Magical Gardens

Denver Region

Text and photography by
Maureen Jabour

Illustrations by
Drew Thurston

WESTCLIFFE PUBLISHERS

bigearthpublishing.com

Dedication

For my husband, Chris,

the Assistant Gardener;

our grandchildren,

Nicholas and Lauren;

and for Louise Lavender Rouse

and Barbara McColley Cohen

Acknowledgments

To Evalyn McGraw,

who transcribed and edited the manuscript

To Tom Gillam,

owner of Native Nursery, and his foreman, Jesus Calderon,

for their excellent work

To publisher Linda Doyle

To designer Rebecca Finkel

To Westcliffe editor Ali Geiser

and

Special acknowledgment to

Mike Eagleton and Barbara McColley Cohen

Contents

Introduction

A friend bewailed the fact that she was moving from Los Angeles to Denver and, as she was a keen gardener, was despondent that her gardening days were over. This book should disprove her theory.

These magical retreats are places of enchantment, a tribute to the gardeners and garden designers who have seen their dreams come to fruition. Like a jewelry box brimming with gems, the photographs will delight and inspire any neophyte gardener.

Gardening, however, is not all froth and frivolity or strolling airily in a picture hat; it takes hard work and dedication. There is no such thing as a maintenance-free garden. This canard is equal to the reassurances of nurses on a maternity ward who tell the new mother, "Your baby always sleeps through the night," or to the hoary story of the car salesman who says, "This car was owned by a little old lady who used it only to drive to church on Sunday." Every garden, no matter how simple its style, requires maintenance.

Gardening should be an enjoyable hobby (or obsession), not a burden to be dreaded. Take the time to sit in the garden, reflect on the play of sun and shadows on the lawn and beds, and breathe in the delicious scents of flowers, herbs, and newly mowed grass.

Take a moment or two to study the activities of the inhabitants of your patch of Eden: butterflies floating; bees nuzzling snapdragons, their bottoms waggling cheekily; the pale green, sinister-looking praying mantis stalking its victims; and finally, that most welcome visitor, the hummingbird, hovering above physostegia and agastache.

This book is an excursion through some of Denver's most unusual and colorful gardens—small, medium, and large. Shrubs, perennials, bulbs, and annuals live in clever harmony to delight the most discerning eye. Gardening is an absorbing hobby, and those who indulge in it devote much time and effort pursuing perfection. Gardeners are a generous lot, willing to share their knowledge with other like-minded devotees.

The fraternity of gardeners creates a special bond among its members, as people of all ages and from all walks of life mingle happily, for in gardening there are no class barriers. Even in the United Kingdom, where there are still some class distinctions, gardening is the great equalizer. At garden shows and tours, aristocrats mix with artisans, dukes hobnob with doctors, and marchionesses make merry with maids as they all discuss their favorite pastime—gardening. If you are able to tell the difference between a pelargonium and a geranium, or identify clematis 'Jackmanii' and clematis 'Nelly Moser,' you are welcomed into the club.

My mother used to say, "Rome wasn't built in a day." So here are words of advice I pass along to my California friend: Look at these Denver gardens, then roll up your sleeves and, with spade in hand, get to work. You will be rewarded with the satisfaction of knowing not only that you have created something worthwhile and special, but that you have joined the ranks of Denverites who aim to beautify their neighborhoods and to give joy to their families and friends.

CHAPTER ONE

Small Gardens, Courtyards, Patios, and a Victorian Porch

BILL & SARAH
Weeks
CHERRY CREEK NORTH

*Plants featured in this section include: tulips, daffodils, pansies,
hyacinths, bedding dahlias, verbena, petunias, and impatiens*

Sarah's garden demonstrates the best possible use of limited space. This darling little townhouse garden draws passersby like a magnet. They stare in wonder at the beauty created by Sarah and the Garden Gals, Skye Mason and Jessie McVay. Not only are Skye and Jessie knowledgeable and experienced, their choice of color combinations and plantings makes this jewel of a garden memorable. They take great pride in maintaining the garden in its immaculate condition.

In the spring, the 15-by-20-foot front garden is a mass of differently hued tulips, purple pansies, and purple hyacinths. A bed carved out near the corner of the sidewalk is filled with tulips, daffodils, and pansies, while the entire 1-by-100-foot sidewalk bed is crammed with tulips. The *tout ensemble* is a tulip-lover's delight. In summer, the colors intensify when lavishly planted magenta and pink impatiens add to the visual excitement.

Sarah has definite ideas about how her garden should look. She is partial to the English style of separate, formal areas, each one furnished with an uncluttered and distinctive design. A fountain, which splashes into a pond, dominates the entrance courtyard, where a bench provides a peaceful spot from which to view the exuberant show.

An iron gate leads into the second courtyard, where seating is arranged around an inviting fireplace. Luxuriant plants cascade from five magnificent window boxes positioned on the second-floor wall of the house, lending the area, where the family may relax in complete privacy, a European flavor. A short passage leads to the third courtyard, which is used for dining. Doors from the house lead out to both courtyards, allowing the Weeks to entertain large numbers of guests in the cleverly planned spaces.

Every available inch of this property is utilized; even in the narrow passages, tomato plants are trained to grow against an iron grille, while an herb patch is squeezed into remaining space.

Sarah was raised in Abilene, Texas; her loyalty to that state is matched only by her love of Colorado and its majestic mountains. She breeds rare Rocky Mountain horses on her farm, 8th Heaven Horse Farms, in Castle Rock. She and her husband Bill gain tremendous satisfaction and joy when they gaze at the abundance of brilliant color in this magical little garden in Cherry Creek North.

CREDITS

**Don Dashney, Interior Designer
(Stewart-Williams):**
    Window boxes in second courtyard
    Outdoor decorating in second and
      third courtyards
    Pond and fountain design

**The Garden Gals, Skye Mason
and Jessie McVay**
    Garden design, planting, maintenance

TERRY
Vitale
ENGLEWOOD

Plants featured in this section include: tulips, campanula, petunias, and zinnias

I s there anyone in Denver busier than Terry? She owns and publishes *Colorado Expression, Architecture & Design of the West,* and *Confetti* magazines. She hosts numerous parties and charity events, cooks superb meals, entertains her grandchildren, and yet finds time to attend to her charming garden.

Terry raised her family in the house she has lived in for 34 years. The containers, perennials, and annuals—and especially the private rear garden where she loves to entertain friends and relatives—give credence to Terry's attachment to her garden.

In early summer, exquisite red roses clamber over the mailbox, giving a hint of the delights to follow. Lushly planted containers lead to a side passage and the secluded rear garden. Instead of a lawn, flagstone and brick paving create a generous space for entertaining. Colorful beds border the patio, while containers ablaze with annuals are grouped strategically around the area. In early summer, blue campanula and anemone surround "Community," an unusual steel art sculpture. Numerous shrubs and trees ensure that this little Eden remains private.

The patio is divided into two sections; one side is dominated by a beautifully designed fireplace and comfortable seating (Terry's outdoor sitting room), and the other is a dining area adjacent to a flowerbed crammed with colorful zinnias, rocket snapdragons, and Victoria salvia.

Terry plans her beds carefully, each year making notes in her journal about which plants have been the most successful. She truly loves her garden and, in good weather, can be found planting, weeding, and deadheading. Her garden, cooking skills, and warm, generous spirit reflect the passion inherent in her Italian heritage. Her priorities are her family and friends, her publishing business, and the numerous charitable activities in which she participates.

TERRY *Vitale*

13

Washington Park is an area much sought after by those who wish to live in the city near all its amenities, yet still have a hankering for a small garden. In spring, Matt and Mike's sidewalk garden is one of the prettiest in Denver. They designed and installed the garden over a period of two years until it finally was finished to their satisfaction. Matt's love of gardening is an inheritance from his mother, while his father taught him the art of pruning.

Matt and Mike are both avid gardeners determined to create a tapestry of pink, white, yellow, and blue low-growing perennial groundcovers in place of a lawn. They have succeeded, for the tapestry, when in bloom, is exquisite. The brilliance of their design and the hard work involved are apparent as one views the 120-foot length of the garden.

Yellow and pink ice plant, white snow-in-summer, lilac thyme, and myriad other groundcovers glow as onlookers marvel at the ingenious design and brilliant colors. The 6-foot-wide strip adds a dash of pizzazz to the entire block.

A lovely brick wall encloses the corner property, ensuring privacy in the small rear garden and patio. An 18-inch-wide bed of pink 'Betty Prior' roses, complimented by sharp green thuja and the tracery of Boston ivy, breaks up the starkness of the wall. In the front of the house and leading to the front door, Matt and Mike carved out beds, filling them with black-eyed Susan, phlox paniculata, heuchera, cranesbill 'Johnson's Blue,' and roses.

A simple, yet elegant, design defines the back garden. Narrow beds filled with perennials and roses encircle a small lawn; in mid-summer feverfew bursts into a mound of gleaming white flowers. A grapevine clambers over an arbor built at the perimeter of the property.

Beneath the arbor, the two indefatigable gardeners installed a water feature--a fountain from which water streams into a pond. They found mosquitoes to be a problem in the summer, but solved that by adding goldfish, which eat the larvae. They bring them into the house to overwinter (the goldfish, not the mosquitoes).

Matt and Mike have overlooked no detail in their quest to create this gem of a garden. Owners of small city gardens would do well to emulate what these two hardworking gardeners have accomplished—a garden that inspires neighbors and friends. It is "sidewalk heaven."

Some of Matt and Mike's Sidewalk Groundcovers
Veronica repens 'Sunshine'
Hypericum
Candytuft
Sedum 'Dragon's Blood'
Ice plant 'Table Mountain'
Soapwort
Thyme 'Pink Chintz'
Sedum 'Coral Carpet'

Plants featured in this section include: Rosa 'Betty Prior', yellow sedum, ice plant 'Table Mountain', Rosa Morden 'Fireglow', coral bells, grape vine, and garden phlox

MATT *Claussen* & MIKE *Ciampa*

ROBIN & DIANE

Smith

GOLDEN

Plants featured in this section include: dwarf marigolds, petunias, zinnias, blue lobelia, 'Blue Mist' Spirea, Asian lilies, 'Karl Foerster' feather reed grass, climber Rosa 'America', and dwarf Alberta spruce

This charming garden is the work of an avid gardener who, over several years, has created a magical cottage garden. Diane must have green thumbs, for everything she plants seems to thrive. She and Robin manage the 0.25-acre lot with no help: Robin mows the lawn, digs the holes for the shrubs, and generally t

akes instruction from Diane. He has the patience of Job, for Diane continually changes the design of the beds and moves the shrubs so that Robin and his spade are constantly at work.

Diane is self-taught and, during the 14 years the pair has lived in the house, has developed a keen eye for color patterns, which makes this garden so delightful. The house, situated atop a hill, has a view of the foothills from the rear garden.

A lovely mixture of cosmos, snapdragons, petunias, lobelia, and dwarf marigolds fills a semi-circular bed in front of a brick planter. A few perennials—yarrow and Shasta daisies—grow as well, but Diane prefers to rely on annuals for their dazzling displays that last all summer.

The brick planter at the rear of the bed spills over with salvia, zinnias, lobelia, and petunias. A small waterfall and pond next to the house and overlooking the patio was constructed by the tireless Robin. A narrow planter bed edging the pond is also filled with jewel-like annuals, including dwarf marigolds, petunias, and lobelia. A magnificent clematis 'Jackmanii' adds to the patio's charm.

Red and pink climbing roses cover two iron arbors that lead to a second patio also enclosed by a brick planter filled with a seasonal display. Diane uses unusual containers: a wheelbarrow, an old tin receptacle, and an iron spiral stand which supports four pots filled with annuals. Diane and her stalwart assistant Robin have created a lovely cottage garden which may serve as an example for anyone desiring to make changes in his or her own garden.

NED & BETSY

Kirschbaum

LITTLETON

Plants featured in this section include: impatiens, petunias, Shasta daisies, 'Karl Foerster' feather reed grass, green sweet potato vine, begonias, fuchsia, black-eyed Susan, sedum 'Autumn Joy', day lilies, 'Blue Mist' Spirea

Six aspen trees surrounded by glittering magenta-colored impatiens stand guard at the shady, sandstone-paved entrance to the Kirschbaum house. The courtyard's understated contemporary elegance and pleasing symmetry is enhanced by the repetition of impatiens encircling a striking column of black granite which is, in fact, a fountain; water burbles from its top and slides down its glistening sides. Green potato vine, salmon-colored begonias, coral fuschia, and lime green coleus fill four tall oriental urns. The combination of trees, fountain, splashes of magenta impatiens, and the dramatic impact of the urns gives the courtyard an air of sophisticated harmony.

Ned and Betsy have lived in their house for 12 years; 3 years ago they decided a radical change was needed. They called on landscape designer Mike Eagleton to redesign both the courtyard and the back garden. He incorporated ideas from Ned and Betsy—two avid gardeners—who were open to all suggestions.

Situated on a ridge, the back garden and patio overlook tree-filled Horsemen's Park. A 70-foot curved bed was carved out adjacent to the patio and filled with Shasta daisies, black-eyed Susan, sedum 'Autumn Joy,' and calamagrostis 'Karl Foerster' feather reed grass. The bold color of magenta impatiens edges this lovely, easy-to-maintain bed. The unobstructed view of the verdant valley below combined with the vibrant bed of perennials makes the patio a delightful area in which to entertain or just relax. Together, Mike, Ned, and Betsy have created an exciting contemporary garden—one that will give them pleasure for many years to come.

CREDITS
Mike Eagleton
Landscape designer

BILL & LOUISE
Barrett
CHERRY CREEK NORTH

Plants featured in this section include:
geraniums, petunias, tulips, hyacinth, and impatiens

In spring, lured to Bill and Louise's delightful front garden, passersby admire the show of red and yellow tulips that fill every inch of available space. Alliums' rounded heads add to the viewing enjoyment, as do the classical urns overflowing with pansies.

For her summer garden, Louise also prefers bright colors, and chooses perfectly for the small spaces. Reaching its peak in August, the garden is alive with pink and purple petunias, red geraniums, and magenta-hued impatiens, forming a brilliant mosaic. Flagstone pavers allow for easy maintenance.

The 50-by-25-foot courtyard is spacious enough to support beds on either side of a brick path that leads to a vine-covered arbor under which sit a table and chairs. Even in the heat of a summer's day, this area is cool and welcoming, affording the ideal vantage point from which to view the vivid plantings. Under the dappled shade of a catalpa tree, magenta impatiens light up the area. Surrounded by scarlet geraniums and a bed of pink petunias, a unique fountain acts as a striking focal point.

Bill and Louise derive much satisfaction and pleasure from their little Eden, hidden from the outside world by 6-foot walls and the shelter of the house. A charming garden deserves charming owners—and in this Cherry Creek North garden, the match is perfect.

CREDITS
The Garden Gals, Skye Mason and Jessie McVay
Planting and maintenance

GARY & JOYCE
Pashel
DENVER

Plants featured in this section include: boxwood, sweet potato vine, petunias, begonias, and climbing rose 'Sally Holmes'

Despite the bustle and traffic of one of Denver's busiest areas, Gary and Joyce's house is situated on a quiet street where they have resided for 30 years. Joyce, a ceramics artist whose work has been featured in several magazines, is also a talented and avid gardener. Her exceptional designs are apparent in the two beautiful courtyards where every detail has been carefully thought out; her true artistry is demonstrated by the restrained elegance of the black and white chair coverings and her inventive grouping of urns.

Low boxwood hedges edged with white begonias line the brick-paved entrance courtyard; boxwood also encircles a splashing fountain. Two lushly planted urns frame the front door.

The spacious courtyard at the rear of the house features an espaliered apple tree planted by Joyce against the wall of the house. White petunias fill a trough that rests on an iron support. Groupings of urns and containers overflowing with annuals continue the white theme favored by Joyce; touches of orange begonias make a lovely contrast. The luminous white flowers are especially effective at dusk.

Sparkling water bubbles from a three-tiered fountain, and the climbing rose 'Sally Holmes' provides an idyllic background to this charming grouping. Prolific use of lime-hued sweet potato vine adds vibrancy to this stylish scene. A grapevine climbing up and over the supports of the pergola creates a leafy retreat. Under this canopy, there is a Colorado marble table large enough to seat 10 guests. At night, twinkling lights add to the magic of this lovely setting, which is reminiscent of a courtyard in a Roman villa.

CREDITS
The Garden Gals, Skye Mason and Jessie McVay
Maintenance, pruning, and clipping shrubs

DORIENNE
Jabour
CHERRY CREEK NORTH

Plants featured in this section include: zinnias, black-eyed Susan, cosmos, and marguerites

Much thought, planning, and ingenuity went into making this courtyard as private as possible. To solve the privacy issue, as well as to enhance the appearance of this enchanting space, Dorienne erected a 10-foot-high arbor against the fence. Ivy creeping up the fence and framing an antique wall fountain, plus a plethora of lush plantings, has resulted in a charming tableau in this surprisingly generous 25-by-20-foot sandstone-paved area.

The 'Sally Holmes' climbing rose, though only two years old, has already grown to a height of eight feet, smothering the supports of the arbor in a shower of creamy blooms. An 18-inch-wide rock planter built lengthwise against the 120-foot fence allows Dorienne to plant an array of shade plants, including hostas, ferns, and impatiens; in the sunny area, black-eyed Susan, marguerite, and cosmos thrive.

Dorienne's inventiveness and skillful planning has transformed this area into a delightful outdoor room, demonstrating, as well, how privacy can be achieved despite the proximity of neighboring houses.

JOHN "CHIP" & LEE-ANN

Krauss

CHERRY HILLS VILLAGE

Plants featured in this section include: petunias and roses

Chip and Lee-Ann's patio is notable for its magnificent 30-foot rose bed, which blooms for two months and provides a festive backdrop. The containers, kept in pristine condition by daily deadheading and snipping by Lee-Ann, brim over with purple, pink, and red petunias—a glorious combination. They augment the beauty of the 30-by-15-foot patio, an ideal spot for outdoor entertaining.

FRED JR & FREDDIE III

Gluck

BOULDER

Plants featured in this section include: sweet potato vine, coleus, black-eyed Susan, and 'Karl Foerster' feather reed grass

The following is a recipe for creating a beautiful garden:

Take one determined and keen gardener
Add a large dollop of perfectionism
Sprinkle in enthusiasm and a quest for further plant knowledge
Throw in a million-dollar view
Briskly stir all ingredients
Result: a perfectly manicured lawn, sans weeds and disease,
*   and immaculately maintained beds.*

An Italian mosaic dining table, black iron chairs, wooden benches, and bold container plantings of elephant ears, coleus, and sweet potato vines furnish the spacious sandstone-paved patio. Fred and his son Freddie have an unimpeded view of the magnificent Rocky Mountains from the patio, where they enjoy the garden most. This delightful patio is a peaceful retreat of sophisticated charm.

CREDITS
Monica Tymaio,
Higher Ground Gardens
Maintenance

MIKE & ROSEANN GEIGER-

Paslay

EVERGREEN

Plants featured in this section include: larkspur, cornflowers, poppies, and other wildflowers

The wraparound porch of the Victorian-style house built by Mike and Roseann provides an uninterrupted view of a forest of magnificent pines and aspens. Instead of planting a lawn or formal garden, Roseann was inspired to turn the front area into a wildflower garden. She scattered more than a pound of seeds on the barren ground, as well as on the steep slope leading down to a stream in front of the trees. In late spring and on into summer, this expanse is awash with red and yellow poppies, lilac and purple-hued larkspur, and blue and pink cornflowers.

In keeping with the Victorian character of the architecture, Roseann furnished the porch with cane tables and chairs, rockers, ferns, and posies of fresh flowers, all reminiscent of a gentler, bygone age—a lovely porch in a lovely setting.

Colorful Beds
and
Containers

CHRIS & MAUREEN

Jabour

GOLDEN

*Plants featured in this section include: Shasta daisies, yarrow 'Moonshine',
roses 'Iceberg' and 'Showbiz', lavatera, clematis 'Jackmanii,' and clematis 'Hagley Hybrid'*

A Remodeled Rose Bed

Fortunate gardeners exist who have the virtues of forbearance and patience—I am not one of them.

My forbearance and patience were severely tested by my rose bed, which is 30 feet by 8 feet. For eight years this bed was my pride and joy, a glorious summer sight of floribundas that flourished year after year and bloomed without fail. Three years ago, I noticed that some of them weren't as prolific as usual, and assumed they needed more attention. So the following spring I pruned, fertilized, fussed, and fumed—all to no avail. Horrid insects within hailing distance descended on the bed: aphids and the leaf cutter bee. Diseases followed: mildew and black spot; then some of the leaves turned a pale green. In a frenzy of activity, I removed several bushes and replaced them with new ones. I added lashings of compost and manure, recalling the memorable words of the Duchess of Windsor who said, "You can never be too rich or too thin—or use too much manure."

I added fertilizer and iron, and there was some improvement, which raised my hopes. These were mercilessly dashed when, last year, many of the stems grew long and skinny, and the weight of the buds, when they opened, caused the stems to collapse. They either lolled indolently against their neighbors or, worse, they lay prone on the ground (which was what I felt like doing).

This disaster added to the many tasks associated with the wretched bed, namely, staking and propping up the offending stems with a heterogeneous collection of sticks and supports. By this time, all this activity was sapping both my energy and patience. I was determined to do something drastic: get rid of the worst of the miscreants and plant perennials in their place.

Roses are notorious snobs; they resent having to share their space with common plants. "To hell with them," I thought vengefully as I planted yarrow 'Moonshine,' Shasta daisies, heliopsis, and, as a final insult, cosmos. The roses would just have to get used to hobnobbing with the hoi polloi.

My Better Half (also known as my Assistant Gardener/Financial Backer) gloomily predicted disaster. "You'll regret this," he said glumly. "Don't say I didn't warn you." My reply echoed that of Clark Gable, who said to Vivien Leigh in the film *Gone With the Wind:* "Frankly my dear, I don't give a damn."

What were the reasons for the peculiar behavior of the roses? To quote Claude Rains in the movie *Casablanca*, "Round up the usual suspects," which are:

1. Too much shade as trees grow taller and their roots sap the soil of nutrients and moisture
2. Voracious insects
3. Diseases
4. Lack of iron
5. A desire to make the gardener crazy and send her into the loony bin

All these reasons were beyond my coping abilities. The rejuvenated bed was colorful for a much longer period; when the first flush of roses was over, the perennials filled in the gaps. The Herculean task was well worth the effort. The Assistant Gardener, who mourned the loss of the roses (he wore a black armband), eventually agreed that the change was for the better.

LLOYD & JODI

Wilcox

GOLDEN

Plants featured in this section include: cosmos

An Annual Bed

What could look more cheerful or give more pleasure to the gardener than a bed of cosmos? This unassuming plant is a workhorse, obligingly flowering until frost. Lloyd and Jodi's beautiful 40-by-6-foot moss rock planter bed is the ideal venue for these easy-to-grow annuals. Cosmos, or Mexican aster, come in shades of white, pink, and a deeper pink. They dazzle and delight as more and more flowers appear as the season progresses. Their ability to drop volunteers is a bonus, ensuring a good crop for the following year.

Lloyd and Jodi are meticulous about deadheading, which encourages sturdier plants and more prolific blooming. This carefree flower gives them much satisfaction and pleasure.

BUELL
Mansion

CHERRY HILLS VILLAGE • ANNUAL BEDS
DESIGNED BY GROUNDMASTERS

Plants featured in this section include: petunias, marigolds, and verbena

CHRIS & MAUREEN
Jabour
GOLDEN • PERENNIAL BEDS

Plants featured in this section include: marigolds, Shasta daisies, black-eyed Susan, catmint, and yarrow 'Moonshine'

Containers

AN ASSORTMENT OF URNS AND POTS

Chris and Maureen Jabour's marguerites and lobelia

Left: Buell Mansion

*Above and left:
Lloyd & Jodi Wilcox's
garden*

73

Colorado's Gardening Newsletter

June 2007

The Monthly Blab

The Gardener's Friend

by Garrulous Gertie

Hiya folks! Have I got news for you! I'm breathless with excitement! Famous gardener Leroy "Tex" Dolt, from Dirtwater, Texas, will be joining the Newsletter staff to help in solving gardeners' problems. He's left his brother-in-law, Duane Hick, in charge of his business, El Risko Nursery/Easy Credit Co., and is confident that Duane will manage the business and keep the home fires burning while he--Tex—is in Colorado. We are definitely going to benefit from his move. In a recent interview on a local television station, Tex said, "I sure am glad to be in Colorado, where a man's a man and he still totes a gun. In Texas we say, 'We like our steaks big, our talk plain, and our women fancy.' Heh, heh."

What a sense of humor! So send in your gardening problems—and welcome aboard, Tex!

Annual Poetry Competition

We at the Newsletter are very excited about this competition. The winner will receive a FREE trip to the Gobi Desert, traveling on Yak-Yak Express Airlines, whose proud boast is that only 60 percent of their planes crash during takeoff. Their well-known slogan, "We accept all animals, including goats and chickens," will come as relief to animal lovers who hate leaving little Fifi in a boarding kennel. A word of warning, however: Small dogs are considered a delicacy in parts of the Gobi, so hold onto that leash!

We also recommend that you bring your own food, as the national dish of goat's liver stew will be served on the plane. Yak-Yak Airlines will serve

Last year's Poetry Competition winner, Dimples Doodler, arriving at Yak Yak Airport.

Teeth Lost in Gust of Wind

A freak wind blew through Colorado yesterday, damaging the well-known vegetable nursery of Hiram Z. Glockenspiel, 88. Hiram, who was milking Daisy the cow at the rear of the nursery, was swept up and, with Daisy, deposited in a neighbor's field. Hiram and Daisy (below) were unhurt. Hiram's only complaint was the loss of his teeth, which were blown out of his mouth by the force of the wind. The milk pail is still missing.

"Me and Daisy sure was surprised to find ourselves in farmer Smith's field," mumbled Hiram when interviewed by a reporter from the *Colorado Bilge*. "We hightailed it back to the nursery thanking the good Lord for sparing us. But what about my teeth? I tried the wife's teeth, but they kept falling out! Now how in Hades am I going to give a speech tomorrow about how to grow a 10-foot-long cucumber without my @#$!& teeth?"

FREE cocktails of fermented camel's milk and crushed nettles, ensuring that you arrive at your destination well and truly plastered.

More advice: Be sure to include a collapsible lawn chair in your luggage, unless you don't mind sitting on the floor of the plane for 18 hours. Only a few seats are available at the rear of the airplane behind the goat enclosure. This is the same area where some of the locals cook to feed their little kiddies.

So put on your thinking caps, send us your poems, and you may soon be on your way to a luxurious hotel and exotic spa in the Gobi!

Gardener's Corner

by Garrulous Gertie

Calling all do-it-yourselfers! This new column will help all of those who want to save money. Our first letter is from Mark Malarkey, who fixed his own fence, saving himself hundreds of dollars! Thank you, Mark. And to all our readers—keep these stories and tips coming!

How to Fix a Lattice Fence

by Mark Malarkey

I woke up last Saturday morning to find that during the night a gust of wind had blown down part of my lattice fence next to the driveway. My wife said she'd call the fence people on Monday, although, secretly, I intended to fix the fence myself. My wife and the kiddies were going to spend the day with her mother, who lives on the other side of town (great news!), which meant she would be gone for at least seven hours. Perfect. This would give me plenty of time to repair the fence without having to listen to any of her advice and nagging. Women! You can't live with them, and you can't live without them. Bless their hearts.

With the little lady safely out of the way, I inspected the damage, which seemed a bit worse than I'd first thought. Two of the posts were leaning slightly to the left and the wood of the lattice was badly splintered. Not to worry. I'd soon have the sucker shipshape. I made a list of what I would need:

Quick-dry cement	Spade
Saw	Industrial-strength glue
Hammer and nails	

I assembled the tools--hammer, spade, saw . . . ? Where's the #$&*@ saw? Haven't I told the wife a zillion times to put the tools back after she's used them? I searched through the entire garage (what are we doing with all this STUFF?), but found only a missing chisel under a pile of 1995 *National Geographic* magazines. I eventually found the saw beneath the pine tree where someone had left it a year ago; it was rusted and unusable. I immediately jumped into my car and, in my hurry, backed into the @*&%# mailbox. I left the debris on the sidewalk and sped to Sam's Surplus Tools/ Body Piercing Parlor and bought quick-dry cement and a new saw.

Back at the house, I dug around the fence posts, mixed the cement in an old salad bowl I found in the kitchen, then poured it into the holes. The posts still seemed to lean slightly, but not to worry, they'd probably settle. The splintered pieces of lattice were easy to stick together with glue and a few nails. I attached the panels to the posts and hammered the nails in firmly. One panel looked a bit crooked, but was easily fixed with some duct tape and glue. That's when a large, jagged splinter pierced my thumb . . . .

When I got back from the emergency room, my wife had returned and surprise, surprise, her mother (that sour-faced bag) was with her. They were inspecting the fence and both had rather strange expressions on their faces. My wife was holding the salad bowl; suddenly I remembered it had been a wedding present from her Auntie Irma. However, it was obvious they realized I had saved a bundle by fixing the fence myself. So I can only say to all you do-it-yourselfers: Go for it; you'll save lots of money!

Gardening News from Around the Nation

by Garrulous Gertie

Great news for all you gardeners who are tired of looking at the same old boring green lawns. World famous scientist Professor I.M. Daft has created a weed-free, black-and-white checkered lawn! His company, Check That Lawn, is located in Cyanide Creek, Arkansas. What thrilling news!

The first lawn was installed at the home of De Witt Cartwright-Cartwright VII in Beverly Hills. Interviewed by a *Piffle* magazine reporter, Mr. Cartwright-Cartwright exclaimed, "My wife Bunty and I are overwhelmed by the positive response from neighbors. We intend to hold a black-and-white soiree which will rival Truman Capote's Black and White Ball–and he didn't have a lawn to match!"

A few snide remarks were heard from such visitors as Sir Marmaduke Poshington of Snobbery Manor in Kent, UK. "Balderdash!" he sneered. "These new-fangled ideas will never be accepted in the United Kingdom." His cousin, Lord Montague Swanky, loyally agreed. "Quite right, old chap. It's all bosh, absolutely!"

These comments were put down to Brit envy and annoyance at the loss of the colonies in 1776.

Colorado's Gardening Newsletter

June 2007

The Monthly Blab

More Gardening News from Around the Nation

More Sensational News!

If a black and white lawn isn't enough to make every gardener's head spin, more scoops are to come. Are you bored out of your skull with those low-growing petunias always being eaten by slugs? Hold onto your hats while I tell you about the latest breakthrough by Austrian biologist Dr. Jawohl Schnitzel, who recently won a prize at the Upper Volta Science Fair. He and his wife—former Miss North Korea Dr. Watta Bute—have hybridized a petunia that will grow to a height of 12 feet! No more slug worries here! A slight setback did occur when Dr. Schnitzel fell off a 14-foot ladder while inspecting the single bloom at the top. Get well soon, Schnitzy!

Another of their experiments, an attempt to hybridize a rose with an extra-strong perfume, was an overwhelming success, despite the fact that several curious bystanders were knocked sideways when thrusting their noses directly into the blooms. Unfortunately, paramedics attempting to resuscitate them also were affected. When interviewed by a reporter from the *Arkansas Daily Scum,* Dr. Schnitzel warned, "If anyvun iss foolish enough to approach der rose vissout a mask, der consequences could be fatal."

Stroking her faint mustache, Dr. Bute said that the rose would be sold with a mask and the telephone number of the nearest emergency room.

The Blab will be selling the rose at a discount, so get out your checkbooks and become the owner of this sensational rose. We'll even throw in an extra mask for FREE!

Even More Gardening News from Around the Nation

Wigless Woman Sues Rock Group

Rocker Slick Slagger, 81, and his group, "The Screechers," are currently being sued by LaBelle Klabber, 87, for the loss of her wig during a concert at the Alabama Nurseryman's Convention & Flower Show.

When the band, who were on their 40th annual farewell tour, switched on their incredibly amplified sound system, it blew Klabber's wig off. The wig flew through the air and was grabbed by an intoxicated teenager, who disappeared with it. Police are making inquiries into the theft.

Mrs. Klabber, who is suing for mental cruelty and replacement of the wig, said, "I was humiliated," when interviewed by a reporter from the *Alabama Sludge.* "Me and my boyfriend here share a birthday, and we couldn't celebrate as usual at the No Hope Bar & Grill."

Her boyfriend, Homer Schnauzzer, 92, was more upbeat. "We're going to sue for a bundle," he cackled, displaying gleaming dentures. "Yessiree Bob, this sure is our lucky day. Now LaBelle can retire from her job at Quik Fix Plumbing/Massage Parlor. We're going to skedaddle down to Vegas and have ourselves a time. And another thing," he added, "Jimmy Carter never would of lost that election if he hadn't of messed around with them Eye-ranians."

Because of recent hip and knee replacement surgery, Slick Slagger was unable to appear in court. He was represented by his attorneys, Grabbe, Grabbe and Snatch, who were confident all charges would be dropped.

Colorado's Gardening Newsletter

The Monthly Blab

Problem Solving

by Leroy "Tex" Dolt

To Tex:

My wife has a bad back, weak knees, an impacted tooth, and an ingrown toenail. Despite these afflictions, last October she planted 500 tulips. This spring, a herd of deer came down from the foothills and ate all of them. Since then, my wife's health has deteriorated and her mental condition is not good. Can you help? —*Distraught*

To Distraught:

Well, pardner, get yourself a 12-bore shotgun with a good scope and let those critters have it right where it matters most. Otherwise, for a small fee, I can put you in touch with a sharpshooter who'll send Bambi and Co. to kingdom come! All our sharpshooters are under 40; oldsters' trigger fingers are a mite shaky for this job. Hope your wife will be better soon, otherwise it'll be the loony bin for her! Heh, heh. —Tex

To Tex:

My mother-in-law, a refined and delicate lady, is visiting us. She and her small poodle Mitzi were sitting on the front porch when a horde of mongrels rushed onto the porch and attempted to molest her (Mitzi, not my mother-in-law). The woman was in shock, especially as Mitzi seemed to encourage the attentions of the brutes. What can I do to discourage these louts and bring peace to our porch? —*Desperate*

To Desperate:

Ask your friendly butcher to save all the offcuts and other assorted rubbish they usually put in their sausages. Boil these for 15 minutes, then stir in one cup Epsom salts, a small bottle of castor oil, and six tablets of that constipation stuff the old codgers use. Place this on the porch for those lowlifes to gobble up. I guarantee you'll have peace and quiet for about a month. By then your mother-in-law and Mitzi will have returned home. —Tex

To Tex:

This spring strange yellow circles appeared in my lawn. My neighbors have the same problem. My daughter's wedding reception is to be held in the garden in August. How can I get rid of these circles? My wife is threatening to have the reception at an expensive hotel if the lawn isn't in perfect condition. —*Worried*

To Worried:

In a large bucket, mix one gallon of kerosene, four cups honey, two large bottles of industrial strength ammonia, a bottle of toilet bowl cleanser, and a pinch of curry powder. Stir well and leave overnight to settle. In the morning, spray the mixture over the entire lawn. Those pesky circles will soon disappear. And hey, congratulations on your daughter's marriage—hope it lasts! —*Tex*

Colorado's Gardening Newsletter

August 2007

The Monthly Blab

Letters to the Editor

Sir:

Re: yellow circles in lawn

I followed the directions given to me by your Problem Solver, Tex Dolt, who seems determined to live up to his surname. I left the bucket overnight in the laundry room, where our prize poodle sleeps. You can imagine our horror when we opened the door to find that our precious Zizi had lost all her hair, bunches of which covered the floor. Yes, Zizi was completely bald! My wife, who does not enjoy robust health, had to be hospitalized for several days. We can only put this disaster down to the fumes wafting from the bucket. Obviously, entering Zizi in the Westminster Dog Show is now out of the question. In fact, both Zizi and I are too embarrassed to even go for a walk outside! The lawns of three of my neighbors who used the mixture have turned a hideous mustard brown. They—and I—are filing a class action lawsuit against your newsletter.

—*Zachariah Z. Zilch, M.D., Ph.D., V.I.P., R.I.P.*

Sir:

We at the EBAPS, or Eat Beef and Pork Sausages, are incensed at your Problem Solver's assertion that we put "rubbish" in our sausages. We use only the best cuts of beef and pork in our products and are proud of our reputation. Legal action will follow if any further defamatory statements are made.

—*B.S. Butts, S.N.R., President, EBAPS*

Sir:

I am the president of SWAT, or Seniors With Attitude. We take exception to your Problem Solver, who has cast aspersions on senior citizens by referring to us as "old codgers," and to his other distasteful comments. We intend to picket outside your offices, and will be joined by SLOP, or Seniors Liberate Oppressed Pets.

—*Mrs. Ruth Blather, President, SWAT*

Sir:

The members of POOP, or Protecting Our Outdoor Pets, were disgusted at your Problem Solver's advice regarding those darling dogs who came onto "Desperate's" porch. They had no ulterior motives and wanted only to befriend little Mitzi, who obviously needed companionship. We intend to take strong action against your newsletter for promoting cruelty to animals, especially our dear four-footed friends.

—*Mrs. Irma Twaddle, Chairwoman, POOP*

Sir:

We at SKRAP, or Senseless Killers Reap Appropriate Punishment, were horrified at Tex Dolt's solution to the deer problem. These defenseless creatures need our protection, and we will continue to picket your offices until this man is hounded out of Colorado. We will be joined in our efforts by our colleagues at SWAT, SLOP and POOP.

—*Mrs. Esther Boloney, President, SKRAP*

Sir:

As a representative of DUMP, or Dummies Understand Marriage Problems, I want to lodge a protest against Tex Dolt's use of the insulting phrase "hope it lasts." Obviously, he lacks respect for the sanctity of the marital state and is an affront to all those faithful couples who have honored their vows for 80 years and more. The loyalty and sincerity of these couples is to be admired, whether it is genuine or not. We are contacting churches and synagogues so that they can take appropriate action.

The lax standards, immoral behavior, decadent living, indecent clothing, coarse journalism, lewd movies, and, most alarming, the high prices of milk and bread show that . . . (*)

—MS. ZENOBIA T. SMIRKE

Sir:

We at SAG, or Seniors Against Guns, were disturbed when Mr. Dolt encouraged readers to use guns to solve their problems. Catapults are the answer. We at SAG have always found that catapults are much more efficient in situations such as those described. It is necessary to have several neighbors lasso the offending deer and then let fly with the catapult. They will flee in terror (the deer, not the neighbors), and the problem will be solved without bloodshed.

While I'm putting pen to paper, I also wish to lodge a complaint regarding the noise our SAG members have to endure. Even when we switch off our hearing aids, the level of noise is still unbearable. The cacophony of teenagers' so-called "music," the oafs on motorbikes roaring down the streets, TV commercials screeching . . . (*)

— R.U. CRANKY

Sir:

We at U.G.H!, or Ugly Grammar Harm's, have read Tex Dolt's column; and are dismayed at his grammatical error's? If this is an example of english usage; theirs' not much hope for future generation's?

—MS; G.A; GAFFE, PRINCIPLE, HAPPY ACRE'S HIGH SCHOOL? AND TREASURER OF U.G.H!

EDITOR'S NOTE: These rambling, incoherent letters have been shortened. Go online to read their additional 30 pages.

Letter from the Publisher to all Subscribers

Due to the avalanche of obnoxious mail we have received, numerous lawsuits being filed against us, and our inability to cope with the thousands of members from SWAT, POOP, SLOP and SKRAP who are picketing our offices, this newsletter will temporarily cease publication. We regret any inconvenience to our hundreds of thousands of satisfied readers and supporters.

Leroy "Tex" Dolt has decided to return to his business, El Risko Nursery/Easy Credit Co., Dirtwater, Texas, where all future correspondence may be mailed.

—IGNATIUS X. SLURPE, PUBLISHER, *The Monthly Blab*

Medium-Sized Gardens

MIKE & KATE
Eagleton
WASHINGTON PARK

Plants featured in this section include: rhododendrons, clematis, hydrangeas, hostas, black-eyed Susan, tuberous begonias, garden phlox, and tree form hydrangeas. Above: Rose of Sharon

MIKE & KATE *Eagleton*

ike, a landscape designer who has designed many of the Denver area's loveliest gardens, has designed his own garden and, as one would expect, the result is perfection. The garden, divided into five sections, consists of an entrance courtyard, a 50-by-15-foot side garden, a patio that overlooks the main garden, a dining area, and a north side area bursting with stunning rhododendrons, ferns, and hostas.

The entrance to his and Kate's Tudor-style residence is distinguished on one side by six Rose of Sharon trees closely trimmed to maintain their distinctive shape; when in bloom, they are showstoppers. Roses, Asian lilies, black-eyed Susan, peonies, and garden phlox fill one side of the sidewalk garden. Impatiens replaces the spring show of pansies on the other side.

A unique iron gate, once a church window, leads into a brick-paved courtyard with boxwood enclosures for seasonal plantings and clusters of containers filled with colorful, overflowing annuals. In mid-summer, several flowering tree-form hydrangeas illuminate the area.

A wooden gate with an arched peephole is the entry into an inviting, cool, and elegant shade garden. The trickling of a fountain surrounded by boxwood and backed by a lattice screen masks the sounds of traffic from the busy street. A massive, wide-rimmed container is stunningly planted with purple potato vine, tuberous begonias, datura, coleus, and impatiens. Mike's treasures—crocosmia 'Lucifer,' hostas, ferns, perennial geranium, Jacob's ladder, foxglove, Japanese anemone, and brunnera pack a long bed. Hostas are important for both form and foliage.

A second water feature is positioned at the end of the bed; the play of filtered sunlight as the water trickles down the large globe affords a soothing effect, adding even more to the enjoyment of relaxing on the patio backed by a 20-foot planter bed which, in spring, is filled with delicately colored pink and lilac pansies. Glowing impatiens, dragon wing begonias, and coleus replace them for a triumphant summer show.

The 30-by-15-foot lawn has a generous bed that is home to azaleas, rhododendrons, hydrangeas, astilbe, daphne, goat's beard, and a white-blooming dogwood. A lattice fence and pergola at the perimeter of the property ensures privacy. Tucked into a corner next to the rear gate, an intriguing classical face from which water flows into a basin comprises yet a third water feature. Ferns, a flower-filled container, and the red leaves of a Japanese maple are visible proof of Mike's inspired design plans; he successfully converted an uninteresting corner into a charming and elegant tableau.

A second planter bed filled with fibrous begonias, coleus, impatiens, and verbena encloses the raised dining area. Opposite, a small bed is shaded by a Japanese maple, under which grow Asian lilies, birdseye veronica groundcover, coreopsis 'Nana,' hostas, and helleborus. A cluster of pots in front of a potting shed adds to the appealing scene.

An area on the north side has been given over to rhododendrons, which, in late spring, provide a breathtaking performance of white and lavender

blooms. Here, in the tranquil atmosphere of this exquisite garden designed by one of Denver's foremost landscape designers, is proof of what may be achieved in a relatively small area.

The Office

The house, where Mike has his office, also has a small back garden. No empty space is safe from his green thumb and fertile imagination. Myriad roses, Asian lilies, daylilies, yarrow 'Moonshine,' daphne, peonies, garden phlox, dahlias, and sedum 'Autumn Joy' fill every inch of space. Hydrangeas, their tiny white florets massed into giant heads, capture the limelight in mid-summer. Asters appear in late summer along with summer annuals, bringing the season to a dazzling finale.

A table and chairs and pots bursting with exuberant colors furnish a small patio which looks onto an arbor festooned with a grapevine and the spectacular climbing rose 'Blaze,' which also smothers a side fence. Adjacent to the arbor, a gate leads into a small enclosure where a Haddenstone *jardiniere* takes pride of place. Filled with seasonal annuals, it is surrounded by larkspur, hostas, brunnera, bleeding heart, and Japanese painted ferns. It is obvious that any garden designed by Mike is a horticultural treasure.

Haddenstone jardiniere

Office plants featured: coleus, Asian lilies, pansies, and roses

TED & NANCY
White
DENVER

Plants featured in this section include: azaleas, magnolia, caladium, torenia, fuschia

Ted and Nancy's Capitol Hill house, designed by architect Harry T.E. Wendell and built in 1889, was remodeled in 1910 and, more recently, by its present owners. The integrity of the architecture remains uncompromised; the house retains its air of solidity and permanence. Renowned landscape designer S.R. de Boer designed the original garden and courtyard fountain in 1900. The garden is reminiscent of Southern gardens in Savannah or Charleston with their dense shade and formal plantings.

Nancy, a writer, consulted landscape designer Mike Eagleton for ideas on how to revitalize the garden. Shade gardens present the designer much more of a challenge than those located in sunny sites. Mike met the challenge, using strikingly planted containers and exquisite fountains as highlights.

In the front of the house, clipped boxwood hedges enclose beds of impatiens—a simple yet effective design in keeping with the style of the house. In spring, a magnolia tree unfurls its glorious blooms, while a pink azalea in front of it bursts into flower, presenting a lovely amalgamation.

An imposing 7-foot-high iron gate opens onto a brick-paved side area where large urns filled with ferns flank a wall fountain. Mike and Nancy resisted the temptation to crowd this space with too many containers; the result is uncluttered elegance. Opposite the fountain is a seating area, above which are window boxes crammed with fuschia, lobelia, begonias, and cyclamen.

A venerable 90-year-old linden tree dominates the main courtyard; a circular bed carved out around it is planted thickly with coral bells, pulmonaria, bleeding heart, hostas, and ferns. Strategically placed classical ornaments add interest to the verdant setting.

Sheltered by an arbor, the second water feature—the de Boer wall fountain—is flanked by containers of caladium, torenia, and fuschia, a pleasing symmetry that adds formality. Clusters of urns and pots at its side are planted with rununculus, cyclamen, and tuberous begonias. Even on the most sweltering summer days, the water features and shade contribute to an atmosphere of order and coolness.

This timeless and magical garden, expertly restored by Ted, Nancy, and Mike, provides the writer in Nancy with inspiration; she and Ted devote their leisure time to maintaining the containers and beds. They should be commended for maintaining—and even improving—this house and garden that is so much a part of Denver's early history.

Right: DeBoer Fountain

JERRY & SANDY
Weigand
CRESTMOOR

*Plants featured in this section include: boxwood, cosmos,
black-eyed Susan, petunias, sedum 'Autumn Joy', and impatiens*

It is difficult to believe that this one-third-acre Crestmoor garden is less than one year old. While the front garden is simple and dignified, it is the back garden that is a place of enchantment and color. Boxwoods are used extensively throughout—shaped into balls, they are especially effective in containers. A 50-year-old locust tree provides shade, while clipped ivy clambers up and over its trunk.

Various perennials reside in a 30-by-10-foot side-bed; annuals in the front add to its exuberance. Sandy chose a shady area at the opposite side of this bed to be a secluded courtyard planted with hostas, ferns, and containers overflowing with glowing impatiens. Moneywort thrives between the cracks in the flagstone, creating an interesting pattern. Who wouldn't want to sit on the white bench among simple shade plants and colorful containers and relax in this magical little courtyard?

An unfortunate hailstorm at the end of June caused damage and heartbreak, but Jerry and Sandy rolled up their sleeves and spent hours cutting back perennials and replanting the containers. With help from a kind friend, Barbara Cohen, they replaced the annuals and, within a month, the bed once more flourished. Jerry and Sandy love their garden, and it certainly is apparent by the immaculate condition in which it is maintained. No weed would dare raise its ugly head to mar the perfection.

A main patio is paved with flagstones, while a wide, brick-paved path and steps lead down to a second patio where the seating looks onto a mermaid wall fountain and pond. The symmetrical design of this area adds to the harmony and charm. London gardens such as this often are featured in English gardening magazines; Jerry and Sandy's could easily grace those pages.

Sandy, an interior designer, chose elegance over excess when she furnished the patios, and worked closely with Denver landscape designer Mike Eagleton to create a superb garden of beauty and serenity.

VERNON & SHARON

Ritzman

APPLEWOOD

Plants featured in this section include: alyssum, marigolds, coleus, petunias, and hen and chicks

Vernon inherited an innate love of the soil from his Iowa farming forebears; gardening is his passion and his hobby. As a teenager, he worked closely with his parents on their farm. He has transferred the lessons he learned there to his life in Colorado. As well as attending to his busy medical practice, Vernon serves as volunteer chair on the board of the Community First Foundation, which has spearheaded fundraising for the Collier Hospice Center and the Breast Care Center at Exempla Lutheran Medical Center campus.

For 35 years, he and Sharon have lived in their Applewood house, which is built on a steep slope where it appears it would be impossible to create a garden. Over the decades, however, Vernon, through ingenuity and tireless work, has fashioned a garden of unusual appeal without compromising the natural beauty of the mountainside.

His first task was building four rock planter beds, each tier 30 feet in length. From mid-summer until frost, these beds overflow with a magnificent display of annuals: alyssum, marigolds, coleus, petunias, and geraniums. An ivy climber growing against a wall of the house has been trained into an intricate pattern, the center of which incorporates a heart, adding to the charm of the vivid kaleidoscope of colors just below it. He makes extensive use of hens and chickens, which grow in between the cracks of the rock walls. Sedum keeps the weeds at bay. Thirty-four shallow steps lead to the deck, where two waterfalls cascade into ponds guarded by a statue of an elk.

Mementos from his parents' farm are found throughout the garden: an anvil, part of a plow, and his father's wrenches, which are embedded into a flat slab of rock. Pairs of old military boots are planted with overflowing alyssum. "An hour in the garden puts life's problems in perspective" is inscribed on two cement books.

The majestic mountains, a towering 40-year-old cottonwood tree, and the colorful flowerbeds all can be viewed from the spacious deck. The soothing sound of the splashing waterfalls adds to Vernon and Sharon's enjoyment as they look upon his labor of love; she has been his constant cheerleader through all the decades of planning and work.

A table and two chairs on an area adjacent to the deck look onto a tree house built by Vernon for their children. It still stands sturdy and ready to be used by future generations. A second set of 20 steps leads to the top of the property. The area where Vernon works, pots, and makes his compost is midway up.

This garden is a testament to the tenacity, imagination, and resourcefulness of an exceptional gardener.

VERNON'S TIP:

"Use water wisely. We are privileged to share with the original gardeners—our farmers and ranchers."

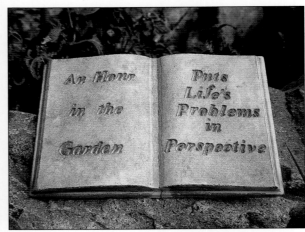

An Hour in the Garden Puts Life's Problems in Perspective

STANLEY & BARBARA

Cohen

CHERRY HILLS VILLAGE

*Plants featured in this section include: petunias, tulips, gaillardia, tanacetum, salvia, roses,
Jupiter's beard, allium, yarrow 'Moonshine', climbing rose 'Blaze', and Asian lilies*

A Tuscan villa comes immediately to mind upon seeing Stanley and Barbara's house. The simplicity and understated elegance of the frontage plantings catch the eye. Six 20-foot-tall, columnar oak trees, immaculately trimmed, line the path leading to the front door. Four stately, 12-foot-tall thuja planted against the house add distinction to the exterior. In summer, pink 'Madison' roses nestled at the base of the trees provide the only splashes of color.

Barbara, a knowledgeable, committed master gardener, volunteered at Hudson Gardens for several years. Her love of flowers and gardening is evidenced by the 0.5-acre garden she created with the invaluable help of Denver landscape designer Mike Eagleton. Guided by Mike, her dream of a wondrous garden has become a reality.

In spring, the 120-foot semi-circular border in the rear garden is filled with a spectacular display of tulips and daffodils, later followed by a stunning show of hundreds of alliums. A statue of St. Fiacre, patron saint of gardeners, gazes on the sea of rounded magenta blooms. Shrubs and trees at the perimeter of the border ensure complete privacy.

Climbers are the dominant feature of the summer garden: Roses, clematis, and trumpet vines grow so tall and heavy that Barbara erected 16-foot-high iron trellises to support them. The red climbing rose 'Blaze' grows to a height of 14 feet, smothering the trellis.

The narrow bed, visible from the courtyard, explodes with Asian lilies, Corsican violets, and geum. The long semi-circular border bursts with exuberant color as yellow yarrow 'Moonshine,' white tanacetum, and a variety of Asian lilies, daylilies, orange gaillardia, roses, and geum jostle for position. This border is never without color, a tribute to Barbara's inventiveness and flair. Generous use of the opulent Asian lily tides the border over during more quiet blooming periods. Velvety-foliaged, bold-patterned coleuses surround an oriental statue, filling a shady bed adjacent to the large border.

STANLEY & BARBARA *Cohen*

The Courtyard

The generous-sized courtyard affords Barbara the opportunity to display her artistry in the form of container plantings. Large urns and pots overflow with atypical combinations of osteospurmum, petunias, lavender, and Santa Barbara daisies. Elegantly shaped boxwood combines with white petunias in stylish urns. Tree bougainvilleas in two large containers provide vertical interest to clusters of pots brimming with luxuriant annuals. A stone fountain enhances the aura of charm and serenity in the center of the courtyard. A red-leaved Japanese maple complements the numerous containers, a pleasing vignette against the blush-colored wall.

Barbara grew up in Southern California, where her mother influenced her love of gardening. When she settled in Denver, the beauty of the Botanic Gardens became a source of inspiration. Mike Eagleton's sophisticated designs captured her imagination and spurred her on to even greater efforts. Her love of gardening is matched by her affection for her four Persian cats and her Havanese puppy. Husband Stanley, a bystander in this ongoing gardening enterprise, admires Barbara's talent and efforts and applauds her from the sidelines.

Barbara's generous spirit, her willingness to share her knowledge, and her infectious enthusiasm make her one of the leaders of Denver's horticultural scene. She looks forward to opening her garden for benefit tours followed by a garden talk and luncheon.

CHAPTER FOUR

Large Gardens

SARAH & KEITH

Grosvenor

DENVER

Plants featured in this section include: snow crab trees, lupine, hydrangea, hostas, impatiens, and ferns

Tucked away on a side street, yet not far from one of Denver's busiest areas, is a gem of a garden whose serenity transports the viewer to a bygone age. Sarah and Keith rescued an 85-year-old house from certain demolition and, with taste and care, restored it and the 0.75-acre garden to their former glory. Sarah, an interior designer, brought her talent and plant knowledge to the project by way of careful planning and design. The result is an enchanting garden distinguished by brick walls, iron gates, flagstone paving, and Sarah's careful choice of garden ornaments. All contribute to the magic of the garden. Traffic noises and the fast pace of the city become virtually unnoticed in the atmosphere of tranquility created by this gifted gardener.

Four blossom-covered miniature snow crab trees guard the entrance to the house in spring. Along both sides of the steps, summer beds are ablaze with red roses. Hostas, Japanese painted ferns, daphne 'Carol Mackie', and astilbe bloom in a shady area along the side of the house. Hydrangeas and sparkling impatiens fill numerous containers.

Draped over the arch leading into the main garden are a climbing rose and sweet autumn clematis. A circular wooden bench built around a shade tree invites one to relax and admire the strategically placed, flower-filled containers and the large east-side bed. Two flowering cherry trees covered with pink blossoms announce the arrival of spring.

Sarah's eye for unusual objects is demonstrated by her whimsical choice of a classical head that lies sideways beneath the foliage of a Japanese maple tree. Plaques, troughs, and unique containers are scattered throughout the garden, each adding its own particular charm.

The Courtyard

The entrance to this secluded area is through a delicately scrolled iron gate. An oriental statue placed against an ivy-clad wall is the perfect accompaniment to the spray from a restful fountain, adding to the atmosphere of peace and harmony. The white clematis 'Henryii' scrambles up the trunk of a tree; baby's breath, sedum 'Autumn Joy,' black-eyed Susan, valerian, and daylilies fill an adjacent bed.

The Containers

Designed and planted by Sarah with the expert help of D'londa Rhoades, owner of Scentimental Gardens, the containers, works of art in themselves, appear in both the courtyard and garden. The garden is a tribute to Sarah's flair, hard work, and her constant quest for perfection. Denver is fortunate to have this enterprising pair, Keith and Sarah, who have devoted their time, energy, and talent into restoring and maintaining a piece of the city's history.

CREDITS

Denver landscape designer Mike Eagleton's expertise and the design ideas and hard work of D'londa Rhoades, owner of Scentimental Gardens, contributed to the success of the garden.

BILL & DIANE

Felsman

BOW MAR

*Plants featured in this section include: moneywort, hostas, bluebells,
hens and chickens, Jupiter's beard, astilbe, sage, roses, and ostrich ferns*

Bow Mar, a close-knit shorefront community located just southwest of Denver, comprises 1-acre lots and a private lake for sailing and fishing. Forty years ago, Diane, a gifted gardener, created her spectacular garden here. The backdrop of the majestic Rocky Mountains enhances the lovely area.

The daunting task of caring for a property of this size was a challenge for Bill and Diane, but they met it with hard work and Diane's clever designs and plantings. Over the decades, she has wrought a miraculous change to what was a bare and uninteresting lot. Instead of a front lawn, Diane filled a huge, 60-by-40-foot bed with valerian, coneflowers, and daylilies. A shady area is home to hostas and ground-covers. Moneywort is planted in between the cracks of the long flagstone path that leads to the front door.

An ash tree, encircled at its base by a bed of hens and chickens, shades the flagstone patio at the side of the house. Bluebells are thickly planted in the flagstone's cracks, generating an unusual and striking combination. The patio faces a 200-by-20-foot magnificent curved border bursting with perennials and roses. It is here that one appreciates the brilliance of Diane's design: a parade of colors—without the brass band.

The lush green fronds of ostrich ferns, complemented by hostas and astilbe, light up a shady area near the house. Daylilies and delicate pink malva continue the show into late summer.

Diane manages this enormous garden with no help; she weeds, divides perennials, digs, prunes, and waters, a never-ending labor of love. The work involved would make the average gardener quake in his or her boots. Bill does his part by mowing the lawn, climbing trees to saw branches, and supporting Diane in all her endeavors.

Diane is both experienced and knowledgeable. Her love of her garden is obvious, as shown by the impeccable state of the huge borders. One can only marvel at her persistence and diligence over the years in managing a non-stop exhibition of colorful beauty. The garden, which has been open for tours and featured in several magazines, is an example of the art of gardening in Colorado.

RICHARD & CAROL
Lillard
LAKEWOOD

Plants featured in this section include: Asian lilies, yellow leopard's bane, Turkish veronica, candytuft, creeping baby's breath, larkspur, climbing rose 'Blaze', creeping phlox, grape hyacinth, columbine, Mexican evening primrose, yarrow 'Moonshine', iris, tulips, bouganvilla, snow-in-summer, garden phlox, and clematis 'Jackmanii'

Rich and Carol, who have lived in their house for 30 years, manage the 0.75-acre property without help. Rich mows the lawn; Carol takes care of the design, digging, planting, weeding, and pruning, working for several hours each day during the spring and summer seasons. Carol has incorporated numerous changes over the decades. Her knowledge, artistic eye, and, above all, her devotion to the garden, are what make it so special. Her restrained good taste in her selection of ornament—birdbaths, benches, containers, plaques, window boxes, statues, and fountains—all contribute to the peaceful atmosphere, adding, as well, a sense of maturity and permanence.

Carol relies on groundcovers to keep the weeds at bay: purple creeping veronica, blue-hued thyme, sedum, phlox subulata, white snow-in-summer, and basket-of-gold. In spring, splashes of color appear: tulips, daffodils, candytuft, and grape hyacinth, followed by waves of irises, peonies, yarrow, larkspur, phlox paniculata, and asters.

A 70-year-old oak tree shades the patio, which looks out onto the garden. Many of the perennials are planted in two 30-foot-long raised mounds, which serve as the focal point.

Trained against the pale-hued garage wall, a spectacular combination of glorious red climbing roses and purple clematis form a pattern around a wall fountain. Two equally stunning clematis 'Jackmanii' planted against the wall of the house clamber to a height of 15 feet. Window boxes ablaze with impatiens, petunias, and lobelia are positioned in between these purple beauties. Carol's sensibilities are evident in her design, color combinations, and flair in choosing just the right weathered ornaments to stage her tableaux.

The Greenhouse

Attached to the house, this 30-by-10-foot room allows Carol to overwinter such tender plants as hibiscus, ferns, pelargonium, and bougainvillea, which, in early summer, she places in various areas of the garden. Even in extremely cold weather, her indoor garden is unaffected. The large south-facing windows keep the greenhouse at an even temperature during daylight hours, while moderate heating keeps the plants warm and comfortable at night.

The Vegetable Bed

An attractively laid out, 30-by-30-foot circular bed, intersected by bricks for easy maintenance, flourishes with a well-tried repertoire of Carol and Rich's favorites: carrots, beets, beans, tomatoes, lettuce, and cabbages. Dahlias, zinnias, and asters provide splashes of color. Cannas, which bloom in mid-summer, thrive in the center of this cornucopia.

With no sprinkler system in the garden, Rich waters the lawn manually with well water. He spreads a truckload of compost from Timberline over the beds in spring. The mulch keeps the weeds at bay, conserves water, and provides nutrients to the soil.

A talented craftsman, Rich built all the gates as well as the charming wooden bridge which spans a small stream at the bottom of the garden. Until a year ago, he also kept chickens, whose fresh eggs he offered to visitors. The chickens are now a dim and distant memory, but the henhouse has become a tool shed. Rich fashioned concrete rocks, cemented them onto the outside walls, and *voila!*—another unique feature in the garden was born.

With the hard work and support of her husband, Carol, a tireless and gifted gardener, has created a splendid and memorable garden.

Above: The greenhouse

MARK & SALLY

Murray

GREENWOOD VILLAGE

Plants featured in this section include: garden phlox, hydrangeas, sea pink, tulips, painted daisies, day lilies, bee balm, impatiens, liatris, Red Hot Pokers, and peonies

Nearly 40 years ago, Mark and Sally purchased land in Greenwood Village and built their house. Over the years, a magnificent garden has evolved. Not many people would be able to cope with a garden this size, but Sally is more than equal to the challenge. She managed all the work by herself for decades, but now accepts help with the planting and maintenance. Sally has strong preferences about the color of the plants she grows, and she seldom uses yellow, finding it too dominant for the palette she favors. Each morning, she strolls through the garden, pinching, snipping, and observing the progress of her perennials. She loves looking at the buds forming, and eagerly anticipates their opening. The beautiful results of Sally's design ideas, skill, flair, and plant knowledge make this garden a joy to view.

Simplicity defines the area in the front of the house. Aspen trees are underplanted with daphne, columbine, bleeding heart, vinca, and fern groundcovers.

At the rear of the house, a stunning long border dominates the Long Garden, which easily takes its place with those seen in celebrated English gardens. The 120-by-30-foot border curves gracefully toward the private lake, which may be viewed from the three patios that lead from the house. The border blooms from spring until late summer, an enviable feat of clever planning. Repeated use of the plants lends a rhythm to the border. The richness and intensity of the plantings is a triumph of the gardener's skill.

In spring, hundreds of red, coral, pink, and orange tulips light up the border. They are joined by brilliant blue forget-me-nots and brunnera—the *tout ensemble* a breathtaking sight. The bold red and pink spikes of lupines, daylilies, Red Hot Pokers, and drifts of bee balm follow. These waves of perennials are carefully planned so that no month goes by without the expectation of more to come.

In the first week of August, the garden reaches the height of its beauty: tiger lilies, bee balm, liatris, and mounds of phlox paniculata take center stage, followed by a *grande finale* of brilliant asters and dahlias. The cast of this dramatic show deserves a standing ovation, with a special curtain call for the director, Sally.

The Moon Garden

Influenced by the White Garden of Vita Sackville-West and Sir Harold Nicholson at Sissinghurst, Sally carved out a 30-by-20-foot area in which she plants white perennials and annuals. The Moon Garden, so called because of its crescent shape, is filled with pansies, peonies, Japanese iris, lupines, phlox paniculata, and hydrangeas. An uncommon brick enclosure designed by Sally features a pattern of Scottish moss and white impatiens; an edging of lobelia and English ivy makes this a striking sight. Containers filled with white impatiens continue the theme, which may be viewed from the adjacent patio.

The Woodland Garden

Opposite the long border is a woodland area where aspen and pine trees are underplanted with azaleas, daylilies, Jacob's ladder, and hydrangeas. A bench provides the ideal spot from which to view the lake and, across the broad expanse of lawn, the long border. In spring, wildflowers and irises cover the lake's farther bank, while ducks paddle across the water. A fireplace and seating area within a secluded courtyard leads to a delightful water feature—a wall fountain that splashes into a pond surrounded by boxwood and colorfully filled containers.

This talented gardener has very decided ideas about which plants to feature and how the overall garden should appear. Reading the histories of renowned English gardeners and garden writers enhanced Sally's already extensive knowledge. She was aided by Denver landscape designer Mike Eagleton, whose experience and sophisticated design ideas contributed to the creation of this garden. Mark and Sally preside over a dream garden exceptional to the Denver area. This is truly a garden for all seasons.

Left: The Moon Garden

ISBN: 978-1-56579-599-0

TEXT AND PHOTOGRAPHY:
© 2008 by Maureen Jabour. All rights reserved.

COVER PHOTO: Mark & Sally Murray's garden
PAGE i PHOTO: Stanley & Barbara Cohen's garden
PAGE ii PHOTO: Mike & Kate Eagleton's garden

EDITED BY: Evalyn McGraw
DESIGNED BY: Rebecca Finkel

PUBLISHED BY:
Westcliffe Publishers,
a Big Earth Publishing company
3005 Center Green Drive, Suite 220
Boulder, Colorado 80301

9   8   7   6   5   4   3   2   1

PRINTED IN China by Hing Yip Printing Co., Ltd.

LIBRARY OF CONGRESS CATALOGING-IN-PUBLICATION DATA
Jabour, Maureen.
  Denver Magical Gardens / by Maureen Jabour.
    p. cm.
  ISBN 978-1-56579-599-0
  1. Gardens—Colorado—Denver. I. Title.
  SB466.U6D458 2007
  712'.60978883—dc22
                                                2007050278

For more information about other fine books and calendars from Westcliffe Publishers, a Big Earth Publishing company, please contact your local bookstore, call us at 1-800-258-5830, or visit us on the Web at **bigearthpublishing.com.**

The author and publisher of this book have made every effort to ensure the accuracy and currency of its information. Nevertheless, books can require revisions. Please feel free to let us know if you find information in this book that needs to be updated, and we will be glad to correct it for the next printing. Your comments and suggestions are always welcome.

John & Lee-Ann Krauss' garden